Father, Hear My Psalms

for times of prayer and praise

Peggy McMahon

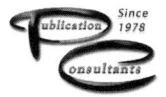

Copyright 2011 by Peggy McMahon
~ First Edition ~

~ Also by Peggy McMahon ~
Abba Hear My Prayers, for times I cannot pray myself

All rights reserved. However these psalms may be shared and reproduced for personal use.

Scripture quotations marked NIV are taken from the Holy Bible, New International Version®. Copyright © 1973, 1978, 1984 Biblica®. Used by permission of Zondervan. All rights reserved.

Scripture quotations marked TNIV are taken from the Holy Bible, Today's New International Version®. Copyright © 2001, 2005 by Biblica® All rights reserved worldwide.

Scripture quotations marked NLT are taken from the Holy Bible, New Living Translation, copyright © 1996, 2004. Used by permission of Tyndale House Publishers, Inc., Wheaton, Illinois 60189. All rights reserved.

Scripture quotations marked NASB are taken from the New American Standard Bible®, Copyright © 1960, 1962, 1963, 1972, 1973, 1975, 1977, 1995 by The Lockman Foundation. Used by permission.

Scripture quotations marked KJ21 are taken from the 21st Century King James Version®, copyright © 1994. Used by permission of Deuel Enterprises, Inc. Gary, SD 57237. All rights reserved.

Scripture quotations marked NKJV are taken from the New King James Version. Copyright © 1982 by Thomas Nelson, Inc. Used by permission. All rights reserved.

Scripture quotations marked KJV are taken from the King James Version

ISBN 978-1-59433-239-5

Library of Congress Catalog Card Number: 2011928699

Publication Consultants

PO Box 221974 Anchorage, Alaska 99522-1974
books@publicationconsultants.com
www.publicationconsultants.com

Printed in the United States of America

*I dedicate this book
to all who hunger and thirst for a greater spiritual connection
and a more
intimate relationship with God.*

~ ∞ ~

In memory of Ken Petersen who sat beside the still waters ...

Cover Photo by Rob Burgess
Seagull Lake, Minnesota

℘ *Psalms* ca

	page
Psalm 23 and the Writing of psalms	9
Psalm 23	13
I Am Not Alone	14
For Times I Feel Lost	16
A Plea for Healing Emotional Hurt	18
In Search of Truth	20
For Courage to Choose the Right Path	22
Seeking the One Who Comforts	24
For Giving My Life to the Lord	26
For Filling My Emptiness	28
For Knowing My Name	30
For Healing of Injury and Illness	32
For Relief of Pain	34
For My Orphan-like Feelings	36
A Prayer for Lifting My Sorrow	38
For Joy	40
For Feelings of Fear and My Need for Protection	42
For Welcoming Strength	44

For Times of Grief 46
A Prayer of Compassion 48
A Petition for Forgiveness 50
For Cultivating My Faith 52
For Hope 54
For My Desire for Love 56
A Prayer for Remaining Steadfast 58
Reflection on Mother Teresa 60
A Prayer for the Poor 62
A Prayer for the Destitute and Homeless 64
A Prayer of Hope for Those Seeking Jobs 66
For the Joy of Motherhood 68
For the Joy of Fatherhood 70
For Celebrating Family 72
For My Desire for Intimacy 74
For My Need for Companionship 76
For Gratitude for Animal Companions 78
A Prayer for Our Children 80
A Vision of Peace 82
For Appreciation of Beauty 84
A Prayer for Honoring the Earth 86
For Raising My Spirits with the Gift of Song 88

Origin of the word psalm:
Old English psealm, from Latin psalmus, from Greek psalmos, from psallein, to play the harp.

The definition of a psalm is a sacred song, hymn, or poem. A Psalm is especially any of the sacred songs by David and others in praise of God in the Book of Psalms in the Bible.

Psalm 23
and the Writing of psalms

Like many of you, I committed to memory Psalm 23. I love its poetic beauty and its sense of speaking directly to me in so many different situations. Over the years I have prayed this psalm hundreds of times; I have prayed it when life has been difficult, and also when life has been joyful. I have prayed this psalm through times of injury and illness, through times of hopelessness and despair; I have prayed to God to turn my illness to healing, my despair to hope. I have prayed this psalm joyfully from mountain tops while picking Alaska blueberries and I have prayed it while sitting on the shore of breaking waves. I have prayed it with gratitude for all that God has given me in my family, my friends, my church, and my animal companions. In all these different times and places the psalmist's words have spoken to me and reassured me of God's presence and abiding love.

I pray the words of Psalm 23 as they are written in the King James Version of the Bible; the words are poetic and beautiful. In Psalm 23 I find the quietude of still water, the rest of green pastures and the peace that comes with reading God's word.

I started to journal as I was praying Psalm 23 and in my writing I began to reflect on the depth of the scripture. I realized that this psalm reflects a universal acceptance of the presence of God in our lives; a God who leads us to rest and peace, a God who accompanies us through dark valleys, a God who provides abundantly for us through His grace. It is a psalm of great faith and I believe it is as powerful today as it was in the days of King David.

In writing my own prayer letters or psalms, I have expanded for me the meaning in God's word. I have put into words some of the thoughts that are present in my mind as I pray the Bible's scripture. The words and the lyrical song of Psalm 23 resonate within me as I create my own psalms that reflect joy and truth and the array of feelings of human nature.

Because I believe the sacred scriptures reflect the mind of God, I do not presume to know the heighth, nor breadth, nor depth of God, for no one can. In writing my psalms, I use my words in harmony with the words of God, so that through scripture my relationship with God becomes ever more intimate. My intent is to share the emotional part of my life which then flows into the spiritual. Out of this flow I experience the connectedness of all things. In the face of strong compelling feelings I sometimes feel untethered, no longer anchored; it is then that I write from my emotions and send them to God so that He may uplift me into the spiritual realm and provide an anchor for me. I would like to share how I integrate the spiritual and the emotional in a rich way using God's word to tell my story. It is my journey to become that story. May God, through these psalms, uplift your soul and bring you peace.

Peggy, June 2011

Psalms for living in Faith and walking in Light

~ ⊗ ~

Psalm 23

The LORD is my shepherd; I shall not want.

He maketh me to lie down in green pastures; He leadeth me beside the still waters.

He restoreth my soul; He leadeth me in the paths of righteousness for His name's sake.

Yea, though I walk through the valley of the shadow of death, I will fear no evil; for Thou art with me; Thy rod and Thy staff, they comfort me.

Thou preparest a table before me in the presence of mine enemies; Thou anointest my head with oil; my cup runneth over.

Surely goodness and mercy shall follow me all the days of my life; and I will dwell in the house of the LORD for ever.
 21st Century King James Version (KJ21)

≈ I Am Not Alone ≈

The Lord is my counselor, I shall not be alone.

He lowers my eyelids during long hours of sleepless black.
He carries me like sacred water
   when I cannot walk beside the still sea.
He lives for me during times of utter collapse;
   He escorts me into the dawn.

He restores my sense of connection,
   He leads me in paths of harmony for His name's sake.

Yea though I walk through the valley of the shadow of despair,
   I will fear no alienation, for your arms, they embrace me;
   they give me courage to walk on.

You prepare a rich oasis for me
   in the presence of my loneliness;
You anoint my head with drops of precious love,
   my cup runs over.

Surely goodness and peace will follow me
   all the days of my life;
And I will dwell in the house of the Lord forever.

Amen.

In her deep anguish Hannah prayed to the LORD, weeping bitterly.

1 Samuel 1:10 TNIV

My soul is in anguish. How long, O LORD, how long?

Psalm 6:3 NIV

I will be glad and rejoice in your love, for you saw my affliction and knew the anguish of my soul.

Psalm 31:7 IV

⁓ For Times I Feel Lost ⁓

The Lord is my pathfinder, I shall not lose my way.
He makes me lie down in meadows of summer bloom;
He leads me to still waters where I drink from His cup.

He restores me in purpose; He leads me to find meaning
   in the smallest of offerings.

Yea, though I walk through the canyon of deepest dark
   I am not lost.
For the light of your heart's love is never extinguished,
   Your nearness is never absent.

You prepare a sanctuary for me in the deep of the canyon walls;
   I receive your true Word.
You anoint my head with belongingness,
   my heart entrains to the pulse of Your heavenly voice.
I hear You call my name and I shall answer.

Surely all courage and direction shall be with me
   all the days of my life;
And I shall dwell in the presence of the Lord forever.

                                          Amen.

Let the morning bring me word of your unfailing love, for I have put my trust in you. Show me the way I should go, for to you I lift up my soul.

Psalm 143:8 NIV

Do not be afraid or discouraged, for the Lord will personally go ahead of you. He will be with you; he will neither fail you nor abandon you.

Deuteronomy 31: 8 NLT

As a shepherd looks after his scattered flock when he is with them, so will I look after my sheep. I will rescue them from all the places where they were scattered on a day of clouds and darkness.

Ezekiel 34:12 NIV

Tears of joy will stream down their faces, and I will lead them home with great care. They will walk beside quiet streams and on smooth paths where they will not stumble.

Jeremiah 31:9 NLT

৯০ A Plea for Healing Emotional Hurt ୧୫

The Lord is my poultice, I shall be soothed.

He makes me lie down in the warm gauze of his healing;
He leads me beside still waters where miracles are born.

He restores my faith, He takes on all hurt,
   He forgives all wrongs.
He leads me in the paths of his calling for his name's sake.

Yea, though I walk through the valley of tears,
   I shall not be overcome, for You walk with me.
Your steady hand and your trusting heart
   keep me grounded in faith.

You prepare a table for me full of loving memories
   in the presence of all my sadness.
You anoint my hurt with the salve of love's salvation;
   You speak to me as your child.
You listen with your eyes, You know who I am,
   You know how I need You.
My blessings are many.

Surely peace and wellness shall be with me
   all the days of my life,
And I shall live in harmony in the house of the Lord forever.
                              Amen.

My grief is beyond healing; my heart is broken.

Jeremiah 8:18 NLT

Thou tellest my wanderings: put thou my tears into thy bottle: are they not in thy book?

Psalm 56:8 KJV

They that sow in tears shall reap in joy.

Psalm 126:5 KJV

Behold, I will bring to it health and healing, and I will heal them; and I will reveal to them an abundance of peace and truth.

Jeremiah 33:6 NASB

ଔ In Search of Truth ଓ

The Lord is my truth, I shall believe.

His Holy book shall be my companion
   as I lay down to rest in God's great garden.
He leads me to the headwaters of His eternal truth;
I am awed by the infinite size of a seed of love
   nurtured by His hand.

He refreshes my mind, body, and soul.
He leads me on the one sure path that will set me free,
   I shall take what God gives me.

Oh, how I long not to be on this arduous journey,
   but to have arrived whole and at peace;
   yet I accept the challenge without fear,
   knowing You leave me not alone.

You prepare a place for me in the presence of all my enemies,
   yet they enter not.
For your truth is like armor and shield to me.
You anoint my spirit with passion,
   my cup spills over into this life and the next.

Surely patience and trust shall surround me
   all the days of my life;
And I shall live in the heart of God's truth forever.
Amen.

Send forth your light and your truth, let them guide me; let them bring me to your holy mountain, to the place where you dwell.

Psalm 43:3 NIV

But whoever lives by the truth comes into the light, so that it may be seen plainly that what he has done has been done through God.

John 3:21 NIV

For we cannot do anything against the truth, but only for the truth.

2 Corinthians 13:8 NIV

Then you will know the truth, and the truth will set you free.

John 8:32 NIV

ೞ For Courage to Choose the Right Path ଽ

The Lord is my sponsor, I shall not fail.

He takes me beyond earthly cravings
  to meadows of sweet innocence;
He leads me beside still water, translucent and pure.
With faults washed away, I am a new beginning.

He restores wholeness to the broken bits of my inner soul.
He leads me in the only path of truth
  and He prays mightily for me.
He hears my groaning too deep for words and
  He turns it into answers of glorious prayer.

Yea, though I walk into valleys flooded with pain, tears and
  brokenness, I will fear no wrong.
You stand steadfast beside me,
  calling my name each step of the journey.
Your voice is pure warmth and love;
  it soothes me through nights of lonely doubt.

You prepare a grand feast for me in the presence
  of all my false gods; You anoint my heart with courage,
  so that I may walk this walk with You.
On days when I have the least,
  my cup runs over with your infinite mercy.

Your grace and your goodness surround me and sustain me;
And I shall live courageously in the house of the Lord forever.

Amen.

Show me the right path, O LORD; point out the road for me to follow.

Psalm 25:4 NLT

I have taught you in the way of wisdom; I have led you in right paths.

Proverbs 4:11 NKJV

Thy word is a lamp unto my feet, and a light unto my path.

Psalm 119:105 KJ21

☙ Seeking the One Who Comforts ❧

The Lord is my comforter, I shall sleep in His arms.

He makes me breathe deeply, when anguish besets my heart;
He leads me beside rolling surf, when my soul needs rest.

He lifts up my spirit.
He leads me in the paths of consoling grace
   for His name's sake.

Yea, though I walk through troubled times, I shall not quiver,
   for your hand and your staff, they steady me.

You prepare a blanket for me under soft skies,
   where I may lie down;
You anoint my head with starlight,
   my breath flows quiet like a river unto the sea.

Surely calmness and peace shall comfort me
   all the days of my life;
And I shall rest deeply in the shelter of the Lord forever.
                                        Amen.

Now a certain man found him, and there he was, wandering in the field. And the man asked him, saying, "What are you seeking?"
Genesis 37:15 NKJV

My sheep wandered through all the mountains, and on every high hill; yes, My flock was scattered over the whole face of the earth, and no one was seeking or searching for them.
Ezekiel 34:6 NKJV

Ask, and it will be given to you; seek, and you will find; knock, and it will be opened to you.

Matthew 7:7 NKJV

☙ For Giving My Life to the Lord ❧

The Lord is my master, I shall give Him my life.

He prays for me as I walk in trails of fiery embers;
   He gives me Holy balm to soothe my fragile skin.
He weeps as I thirst in the hot parched sand;
   He leads me to His oasis, where the desert spring
   is never dry.

He restores my bone dry soul;
He leads me in rain forest paths where I follow
   because He calls my name.

Yea, though I walk through the stifling drought,
   I will not perish, for You have promised everlasting life.
Your word and your promise, they comfort me.

You mold a God shape vessel for me, held in your hands.
You fill it with precious streams that never run dry.
You do all this while anointing my head
   with the tears of the saints.
My outstretched hands overflow with your grace.

Surely You will come for me when my time is finished;
And I will give my life to the Lord, now and forever.

Amen.

Into your hands I commit my spirit; redeem me, O LORD, the God of truth.

Psalm 31:5 NIV

As the deer pants for streams of water, so my soul pants for you, O God.

Psalm 42:1 NIV

Each one should use whatever gift he has received to serve others, faithfully administering God's grace in its various forms.

1 Peter 4:10 NIV

Then I heard the voice of the Lord saying, "Whom shall I send? And who will go for us?" And I said, "Here am I. Send me."

Isaiah 6:8 NIV

ॐ For Filling My Emptiness ☙

The Lord is my water bearer, I shall not thirst.

He makes me take rest on the side of dusty roads;
He leads me beside hidden streams where He bids me drink.

He renews my sense of fullness.
He leads me in paths of rain forest dew, for His name's sake.

Yea, though I walk through the trough of the empty void,
   I will fear no barrenness, for Thou art with me.
Thy hand and thy word they comfort me.

You prepare a bountiful feast for me in the circle of arid plain.
You anoint my lips with water drawn from the banks
   of the rush lined stream.
You comfort me as in the days of baby Moses,
   in the reed made basket.
My gratitude rises in praise.

Surely all love and connection
   shall cradle me all the moments of my life;
And I will live within the Lord's fullness forever.
Amen.

I awaited the dawning of the morning and cried; I hoped in Thy word.

Psalm 119:147 KJV21

It is good that one should hope and wait quietly for the salvation of the LORD.

Lamentations 3:26 NKJV

May the God of hope fill you with all joy and peace as you trust in him, so that you may overflow with hope by the power of the Holy Spirit.

Romans 15:13 NIV

Even the wilderness and desert will be glad in those days. The wasteland will rejoice and blossom with spring crocuses.

Isaiah 35:1 NLT

ॐ For Knowing My Name ॐ

The Lord is my maker, I shall not forget.

He makes me to chant in the chapel of the monks,
   prayers fluttering in the breath of their souls.
He leads me to communion where I drink His holy cup;
He calls me by name, He knows me by heart.

He restores my faith. He leads me in paths of knowing,
   for He has written my name in his heart.

Yea, though I walk through time without knowledge,
   I will fear no evil; for You call me by name,
   your voice and your gentleness, they comfort me.

You prepare a sacred space for me in the presence of absence.
You anoint my mind with wisdom, my heart adores You.

Surely all oceans and seas shall listen,
   and storms will fade when the Lord calls my name;
And I shall know who I am forever.

Amen.

When I consider your heavens, the work of your fingers, the moon and the stars, which you have set in place, what is man that you are mindful of him, the son of man that you care for him?

Psalm 8:3-4 NIV

For you created my inmost being; you knit me together in my mother's womb.

Psalm 139:13 NIV

This truth was given to me in secret, as though whispered in my ear.

Job 4:12 NLT

Let love and faithfulness never leave you; bind them around your neck, write them on the tablet of your heart.

Proverbs 3:3 NIV

"As surely as my new heavens and earth will remain, so will you always be my people, with a name that will never disappear," says the LORD.

Isaiah 66:22 NLT

⊰ For Healing of Injury and Illness ⊱

The Lord is my healer, I shall not doubt His mystery.

He makes me lie down in sleep, His breath upon my cheek.
He leads me beside sacred seas; His Angels they attend me.

He renews and repairs my injured body.
He leads me in the right path of wellness, for his name's sake.

Yea, though I walk through the frightening hollows
 of pain, uncertainty, and death, I will fear no abandonment;
 for You are with me.
Your awesome power and healing, they comfort me.

You prepare a joyful homecoming for me in the presence
 of my trembling; You anoint my wounds with sacred oil.
You cradle my weakened body in the soft warm folds
 of your cloak, You minister unto me.
My cup overflows with prayer.

Surely the love and sacred medicine of the Lord
 shall be near to me all the days of my life;
And I will live in the Lord's care forever.

Amen.

Have compassion on me, LORD, for I am weak. Heal me, LORD, for my bones are in agony.

Psalm 6:2 NLT

Then your light will break forth like the dawn, and your healing will quickly appear; then your righteousness will go before you, and the glory of the LORD will be your rear guard.

Isaiah 58:8 NIV

Then you will have healing for your body and strength for your bones.

Proverbs 3:8 NLT

For Relief of Pain

The Lord is my healer, I shall not doubt.
For in Him, anything is possible.

While I am troubled and in great pain,
   He cradles me like a child in the indigo night.
He leads me into rose colored dawn.

He promises to uphold me in the face of adversity.
He leads me to His word;
   He fills my spirit like water from His well.

Yea, though I walk heavy with discouragement,
   I will not cling to fear.
I will let fear pass, like a shadow under noon day sun.
Your love and compassion, they comfort me greatly.

You make ready a holy place in the presence of my distress.
You anoint my weakness with strength,
   my body wastes not with pain.

Surely your healing will be with me
   through each dusk and each dawn;
And I shall dwell in peace in the hands of the Lord forever.
Amen.

I am in pain and distress; may your salvation, O God, protect me.
Psalm 69:29 NIV

[A psalm of David.] O LORD, hear my prayer, listen to my cry for mercy; in your faithfulness and righteousness come to my relief.

Psalm 143:1 NIV

He will wipe every tear from their eyes. There will be no more death or mourning or crying or pain, for the old order of things has passed away.

Revelation 21:4 NIV

☙ For My Orphan-like Feelings ❧

The Lord is my Father, I shall not want for His presence.

He maketh me to lie down, my head upon His shoulder.
He leadeth me to shelter
  in the calm of the waters running still.
He leadeth me to the well of His heart
  where I shall never thirst.

He nourishes my soul so I stray not from His path;
  His name is holy and is ever on my lips.

Yea, though I walk through the valley of rattling bones
  I will fear no evil, for Thou art with me.
Thy hands shall protect me, Thou leavest me not.

Thou preparest a loving banquet for me in the presence
  of my lost fathers.
Thou anointest my head with healing through sacred oil
  and blessed prayer.
My cup runneth over with love; emptiness I shall know not.

Surely thy grace and thy goodness shall follow me
  to the ends of the earth;
And I will live in the light of my Father forever.

Amen.

The LORD will work out his plans for my life; for your faithful love, O LORD, endures forever. Don't abandon me, for you made me.

Psalm 138:8 NLT

For a brief moment I abandoned you, but with deep compassion I will bring you back.

Isaiah 54:7 NIV

I will not leave you as orphans; I will come to you.

John 14:18 NIV

A father to the fatherless, a defender of widows, is God in his holy dwelling.

Psalm 68:5 NIV

And surely I am with you always, to the very end of the age.

Matthew 28:20 NIV

ஐ A Prayer for Lifting My Sorrow ☙

The Lord is my counsel, I shall run to meet him.

Though I am mute, He gives me strength to cry out
   in the night's lonely storm.
He turns my simple voice into grace filled prayers;
   I ask for His help.

He restores my sense of self; He leads me in paths
   of joyful people for His name's sake.

Yea, though I feel trapped in deep oceans of sadness,
   I will fear no isolation, for You are present.
Your love and your benevolence lift my spirits.

You prepare a joyful seaside table for me,
   where laughter reigns and sorrows fade beyond the breakers.
You anoint my face with many smiles.
My happiness spills softly onto others,
   like water running downhill.

Surely goodness and mercy
   shall carry me over the sea of tears;
And I shall be at home
   in the cheerful countenance of the Lord forever.

                                      Amen.

I weep with sorrow; encourage me by your word.

Psalm 119:28 NLT

You keep track of all my sorrows. You have collected all my tears in your bottle. You have recorded each one in your book.

Psalm 56:8 NLT

He reached down from on high and took hold of me; he drew me out of deep waters.

Psalm 18:16 NIV

Your sun will never set again, and your moon will wane no more; the LORD will be your everlasting light, and your days of sorrow will end.

Isaiah 60:20 NIV

For Joy

The Lord is my joy, I shall not weep.

He makes me run like a deer through the dew at dawn.
He leads me like a child on the edge of the sea,
   skipping stones in a brook running fast and free.

He refreshes my laugh with the rising sun;
He leads me in paths of passion for the awesome beauties
   of this earth.
I sing my love and adoration for His name.

Yea, though I cannot escape all troublesome evil,
   fear will not hold me.
For your ever present gladness walks with me;
   Your word and your promise, they comfort me.

You prepare a feast before me in the presence of heartache,
   You immerse me in joyful baptism.
My life overflows with the bounty of your contentment.

Surely wonder and joy will follow me
   to the far shores of the desert,
   to the white capped dunes of the ocean.
And I will come to You each dawn with joy in my heart
   as I dwell in the house of the Lord forever.

Amen.

They who dwell in the ends of the earth stand in awe of Your signs; You make the dawn and the sunset shout for joy.

Psalm 65:8 NASB

With joy you will draw water from the wells of salvation.

Isaiah 12:3 NIV

Our hearts ache, but we always have joy. We are poor, but we give spiritual riches to others. We own nothing, and yet we have everything.

2 Corinthians 6:10 NLT

For Feelings of Fear and My Need for Protection

The Lord is my protector, I shall not fear.

He makes me lie down in forests of gentle giants;
    He guides me to stand still on running water.
He gives me rest on banks of velvet moss green;
    He shepherds my sleep under soft wings of Angels.

He watches over my soul and breathes new life
    into the worn out sandals of my spirit.
I pray His name without ceasing.

Though I am apprehensive, my fear is overshadowed by trust,
    for You are ever my guardian.
Your shield and your armor, they give me courage.

You prepare a table before me
    in the presence of all my darkest fears.
You anoint my lips with the joyful song
    of the babbling brook,
    the cup of my hands overflows with living water.
You quench my parched spirit and grant me safe passage.

Surely goodness and mercy shall dwell within me
    wherever I journey;
And I will live in the safety of God's house forever.

Amen.

The LORD is my light and my salvation; Whom shall I fear? The LORD is the strength of my life; of whom shall I be afraid?
Psalm 27:1 NKJV

God has said, "Never will I leave you; never will I forsake you."
Hebrews 13:5 NIV

He will cover you with his feathers. He will shelter you with his wings. His faithful promises are your armor and protection.
Psalm 91:4 NLT

You came near when I called you, and you said, "Do not fear."
Lamentations 3:57 NIV

I will lie down and sleep in peace, for you alone, O LORD, make me dwell in safety.

Psalm 4:8 NIV

☙ For Welcoming Strength ❧

The Lord is my rock, I shall know no weakness.

He helps me traverse the narrow blindside of the mountain;
   He deserts me not.
He leads me to storm battered shores; He calms the wind.

He creates me anew with each breath I breathe,
   He summons my name and increases the strength
   of my soul.
For this I loudly sing his praise.

Yea, though I walk through the tunnels
   of the fallen and the weak, I stand unyielding.
For your promise and your presence enfold and uplift me.

You prepare a banquet of nourishment for me
   so I may run and not grow weary.
You anoint me with the hopeful strength of your love.
You, who would move mountains and rocks just to reach me,
   to hold me, to call me your own.
My heart begs for You to hear my thanks.

Surely God's magnificent strength will uphold me;
And I shall live in the light of God's fortress forever.
Amen.

But those who hope in the LORD will renew their strength. They will soar on wings like eagles; they will run and not grow weary, they will walk and not be faint.

Isaiah 40:31 NIV

In the day when I cried out, You answered me, And made me bold with strength in my soul.

Psalm 138:3 NKJV

...For when I am weak, then I am strong.

2 Corinthians 12:10 NIV

ॐ For Times of Grief ☙

The Lord is my Lord, I shall not weep alone.

I cannot sleep, yet He helps me find rest.
I cry out a storm, yet He leads me to safe harbor.

He upholds my soul though it is spent with anguish.
He leads me to those who can carry my pain,
   I only can whisper His Name.

Yea, though I walk through the valley of a thousand tears,
   I shall not faint, for You are beside me.
Though I am small, I am not insignificant;
   your love in this vast universe sustains me.

You prepare a place for my tears in the presence of pain.
You anoint my faith with a vision of heaven.
Though my hurt bleeds raw like a thorn in my side,
   I gather my gratitude,
   so it may flow like an unbroken stream.

Surely healing and wholeness will be born out
   of my mourning;
And I shall dwell in the sanctuary of the Lord forever.
*   Amen.*

The LORD cares deeply when his loved ones die.
Psalm 116:15 NLT

Be merciful to me, O LORD, for I am in distress; my eyes grow weak with sorrow, my soul and my body with grief.

Psalm 31:9 NIV

Surely He has borne our griefs and carried our sorrows.
Isaiah 53:4 NKJV

He has sent me to tell those who mourn that the time of the LORD's favor has come… In their righteousness, they will be like great oaks that the LORD has planted for his own glory.
Isaiah 61:2-3 NLT

You have turned my mourning into joyful dancing. You have taken away my clothes of mourning and clothed me with joy.
Psalm 30:11 NLT

A Prayer of Compassion

The Lord is my friend, I shall be generous.

He encourages me to walk among those who are hurting,
   He leads me beside souls who are broken.

He renews my faith, He places the voice
   of compassion in my words for His name's sake.

Yea, though I walk through the valley of the suffering,
   I shall not turn back.
For You are with me,
   your well of love comforts and nourishes me.

Even though I am surrounded by the hostile and unforgiving,
   You prepare a table before me,
     so I may receive those in need of compassion.
You anoint my head with the tears of the sorrowful;
   my heart opens wide.

Surely a generous heart and a loving Father
   shall follow me all the days of my life;
And I will live among the compassionate
   in the house of the Lord forever.

                                    Amen.

Because of your great compassion you did not abandon them in the desert. By day the pillar of cloud did not cease to guide them on their path, nor the pillar of fire by night to shine on the way they were to take.

Nehemiah 9:19 NIV

The LORD is good to everyone. He showers compassion on all his creation.

Psalm 145:9 NLT

This is what the LORD Almighty says: "Administer true justice; show mercy and compassion to one another".

Zechariah 7:9 NIV

A Petition for Forgiveness

The Lord is my confessor, I shall be forgiven.

He meets me with mercy in the glen of the moss grown spruce.
In contemplative silence,
 He makes me bow down on bended knee.
He leads me beside silent springs of whispering saints.

He restores my soul;
He leads me into deep water lakes
 where my transgressions are washed clean.
I say prayers of gratitude while bathed by living waters,
 within a posture of baptism.

Yea, though I walk through the crowded city streets,
 I shall not waver, for You are with me.
Your constant presence holds me secure.

You prepare life giving gifts for me
 in the presence of all my temptations.
You touch my head with the same sacred oil
 with which You anointed your beloved son David.
My heart spills over with the pure light of your love.

Surely the quiet of the forest and the pureness
 of the spring shall be within me;
And I will live in the Lord's forgiveness forever.

Amen.

As far as the east is from the west, so far has he removed our transgressions from us.

Psalm 103:12 NIV

I, even I, am He who blots out your transgressions, for my own sake, and remembers your sins no more.

Isaiah 43:25 NIV

And He said to me, "My grace is sufficient for you, for my strength is made perfect in weakness."

2 Corinthians 12:9 NKJV

℘ For Cultivating My Faith ☙

The Lord is my minister, I shall not doubt.

He makes me join with his people in universal worship;
    He ministers unto me.
He leads me beside the still soulful water,
    out of which all prayer is born.

He restores my spirit with each rose colored dawn,
    each purple hued dusk.
He asks me to tread in paths of righteousness,
    for His name's sake.
My only desire is to answer yes.

Yea, though I walk through the crowd of nonbelievers,
    I am held fast by faith.
For your Holy covenant rings true like the joyous peals
    of freedom bells.

For hundreds of years You have kept your promise,
    to prepare for me an altar, in the presence of my persecutors.
You anoint my head with sacred Word,
    my heart swells with the conviction of trust.

Surely forbearance and compassion shall follow me
    all the days of my life;
And I will dwell in the heart of the Lord forever.
                                  Amen.

Trust in the LORD and do good; Dwell in the land and cultivate faithfulness.

Psalm 37:3 NASB

O LORD, you are my God; I will exalt you and praise your name, for in perfect faithfulness you have done marvelous things, things planned long ago.

Isaiah 25:1 NIV

I have fought the good fight, I have finished the race, I have kept the faith.

2 Timothy 4:7 NIV

ஸ் For Hope ରେ

The Lord is my savior, I shall not give up hope.

He gives me rest and safe haven;
He leads me to still water, beyond trials of this world.

He fills me from the inside out, so that my very soul
    transcends all despair, and I pray fervently His name.

Yea, though I walk through the valley of loss,
    I will have no fear.
For You fill my heart with the sweet scent of hope,
    and I find comfort in such offerings.

You prepare a grand display for me in the presence
    of all those who believe not.
You infuse my bleakest memory with loving kindness;
    my cup once small, grows full with your abundance.

Surely all hope, promise, and faith surround me
    at every turn;
And I will live in the fullest glory of God forever.

Amen.

Where then is my hope? Who can see any hope for me?
Job 17:15 NIV

Let all that I am wait quietly before God, for my hope is in him.
Psalm 62:5 NLT

This hope is a strong and trustworthy anchor for our souls. It leads us through the curtain into God's inner sanctuary.

Hebrews 6:19 NLT

May the God of hope fill you with all joy and peace as you trust in him, so that you may overflow with hope by the power of the Holy Spirit.

Romans 15:12-14 NIV

ঔ For My Desire for Love ঌ

The Lord is my heavenly lover, I long for His embrace.

He guides me to sit with still ears in the midst
 of His symphony.
He leads me to dance through the singing of the stars.

He refreshes my soul, He leads me in paths
 filled with the essence of love in bloom.

Yea, though I walk through the deep pouring rain,
 I harbor the warmth of your love.
Your hand, reaching out for me is like a cloak upon
 my open heart, a shelter far from the storm.

In the presence of all doubts,
 You prepare a glorious tent in a field full of lilies.
You anoint my brow with the oil of the fruit of the trees;
 love flows from my cup like a river at its source.

Surely the warmth of your sun and the goodness
 of your mercy, shall be my life companions;
And I will live in the love of the Lord forever.

Amen.

Answer me, O LORD, out of the goodness of your love; in your great mercy turn to me.

Psalm 69:16 NIV

Your love, O LORD, reaches to the heavens, your faithfulness to the skies.

Psalm 36:5 NIV

He that loveth not, knoweth not God; for God is love.

1 John 4:8 KJV

And now these three remain: faith, hope and love. But the greatest of these is love.

1 Corinthians 13:13 NIV

༃ A Prayer for Remaining Steadfast ༃

The Lord is my refuge, I shall not hide.

He makes me call out His name
   so I shall know He is there.
He leads me beside the quiet grass of nesting geese,
   so He can soothe my anguish.

He renews my vision so that I can see with clear sight;
   He leads me in high mountain paths of the sure footed ram.
For all His guidance I praise His name.

Yea, though I walk close to the steep of the cliff,
   I will fear no fall.
For your tread is with me.
Whether in front or behind me, your steadfast way
   is the right way; I shall not choose any other way.

You prepare a glorious sunrise for me
   in the fading presence of the darkest night;
You anoint me with golden rays of sunshine,
   my heart sings out in song.

Surely goodness and light shall lift me out of darkness;
And I shall remain steadfast in the house of the Lord forever.
Amen.

Create in me a pure heart, O God, and renew a steadfast spirit within me.

Psalm 51:10 NIV

Look at the lilies of the field and how they grow. They don't work or make their clothing, yet Solomon in all his glory was not dressed as beautifully as they are.

And if God cares so wonderfully for wildflowers that are here today and thrown into the fire tomorrow, he will certainly care for you.

Matthew 6:28-30 NLT

You will keep in perfect peace those whose minds are steadfast, because they trust in you. Trust in the LORD forever, for the LORD, the LORD, himself, is the Rock eternal.

Isaiah 26:3-4 NIV

☙ Reflection on Mother Teresa ❧

The Lord was her life, she gave Him her all.

He made her to serve in the streets of the poor;
He led her beside gutters to seek out the lonely and lost.

He refreshed her soul in the quiet rituals of the masses;
He sent her in the heat of the day to feed hungry souls
   in the name of the Lord.

Yea, though she walked through the alleys
   of the dying and desperate, she held no fear.
For she sought only to bring light into the dark;
   to "see Christ in each of the poor."

The Lord prepared a feast for her
   in the presence of her doubts;
Her cup He refreshed in the midst of a city
   in need of compassion.

Surely she has risen on the wings of the Angels;
And she will live in the house of the Lord forever.
                                       Amen.

I led them with cords of human kindness, with ties of love; I lifted the yoke from their neck and bent down to feed them.

Hosea 11:4 NIV

Do not forget to entertain strangers, for by so doing some people have entertained angels without knowing it.

Hebrews 13:2 NIV

A Prayer for the Poor

The Lord is my provider, I shall not want.

He makes me to walk in the poorest of shoes,
   so I will understand.
He leads me beside creek waters,
   flooded with tears of the destitute and despairing.

He renews my faith in mankind; He leads the sun
   to shine on the least of the poor in His name's sake.

Yea, though I walk through the rubble of alleys
   where the desperate and hungry hide,
I will open my eyes to their need;
   it is upon His table that I lay food and drink.

You prepare a table for the world, where the rich
   will serve the poor and the poor will prosper.
You anoint our poverty with prayer, and our uncertain
   souls with the freedom to choose faith
   in the midst of all our enemies.
The cup You hold is abundantly filled for us.

Surely poverty of body, mind and spirit
   will dwell no more within us;
And we will live in the kingdom of the Lord's riches forever.
                                      Amen.

For I am poor and needy, and my heart is wounded within me.
Psalm 109:22 NIV

If a man shuts his ears to the cry of the poor, he too will cry out and not be answered.

Proverbs 21:13 NIV

Oh, the joys of those who are kind to the poor! The LORD rescues them when they are in trouble.

Psalm 41:1 NLT

All they asked was that we should continue to remember the poor, the very thing I was eager to do.

Galatians 2:10 NIV

๛ A Prayer for the Destitute and Homeless ര

The Lord is our Father, we shall listen to His Word.

He makes us to notice the poor,
    and give shelter to the homeless.
He leads us beside empty waters
    where our presence is needed.

He whispers His promise of compassion;
He leads us to care for our brother who has little,
    our sister who has nothing.

Yea, though we walk through the streets of the wealthy,
    we see the presence of poverty everywhere.
For the sick, the weak and the homeless
    have fallen around us.

We prepare a table for them in the presence of our plenty,
    we anoint their heads with oil.
Our hearts and our hands spill over with compassion.

Surely goodness and charity will follow us
    all the days of our lives;
And we shall dwell in the house of the Lord together.
                                Amen.

The thought of my suffering and homelessness is bitter beyond words.

Lamentations 3:19 NLT

Speak up for those who cannot speak for themselves, for the rights of all who are destitute.

Proverbs 31:8 NIV

For I was hungry, and you fed me. I was thirsty, and you gave me a drink.
I was a stranger, and you invited me into your home.
I was naked, and you gave me clothing.
I was sick, and you cared for me.
I was in prison, and you visited me.

Matthew 25:35-36 NLT

A Prayer of Hope for Those Seeking Jobs

The Lord is my keeper, I shall not despair.

He makes me lie down in the presence of patience;
    He leads me out of dark into the light of His provision.

He restores my hope,
    knowing faith in man follows faith in God.

Yea, though I walk through the winter's bleak cold,
    I will fear no panic, for your guiding hands,
    they comfort me.

You prepare work for me in the presence
    of doubt and uncertainty;
    You anoint my head with plenty.
My cup, nearly empty overflows with the bounty
    of your gifts.

Surely goodness and prosperity shall shepherd me;
And I shall live in the abundance of the Lord forever.
Amen.

But if we hope for what we do not yet have, we wait for it patiently.

                                                              Romans 8:25 NIV

For I know the plans I have for you, declares the LORD, plans to prosper you and not to harm you, plans to give you hope and a future.

                                                        Jeremiah 29:11 NIV

They will neither hunger nor thirst, nor will the desert heat or the sun beat upon them. He who has compassion on them will guide them and lead them beside springs of water.

                                                          Isaiah 49:10 NIV

ঞ For the Joy of Motherhood ଔ

The Lord is my midwife, He has carried and delivered
  me a child.

He makes me hold tenderly the babe of my womb;
He leads me beside legions of ancestors who would
  give up their breath, for the lives of their children.

He renews my faith in family.
He leads me in the path of wisdom so I may learn
  all that my children will teach me.

Yea, though I walk through the valley of all mothers' doubts,
  I will fear no harm, for You are with us.
The doves of your mercy, the lambs of your love,
  they comfort us all.

You seek a christening for all babes,
  in the presence of those who cherish them most.
You anoint our heads and bind us with oil
  from the ties at birth.
We lift joyful praise to the universe
  where You live in all moments.

Surely nurture and blessings
  will fold over us and our children;
And we shall live under the wings of the Lord forever.
Amen.

Your mother was like a vine in your vineyard planted by the water; it was fruitful and full of branches because of abundant water.

Ezekiel 19:10 NIV

A woman giving birth to a child has pain because her time has come; but when her baby is born she forgets the anguish because of her joy that a child is born into the world.

John 16:21 NIV

May your father and mother be glad; may she who gave you birth rejoice!

Proverbs 23:25 NIV

ཥ For the Joy of Fatherhood ❧

The Lord gives me fatherhood, my joy is complete.

He makes me delight in the treasures of my children;
    He leads me beside laughter in the midst of their play.

He restores my sense of wonder;
    He leads me in paths of gratitude for his name's sake.

Yea, though I walk through the valley of all fathers' fears,
    I will not be distressed, for You are with me;
Your promise and grace, they comfort me.

You prepare a shelter of safety in the presence
    of the world's distractions.
You anoint my children with innocence and joy;
    My love overflows.

Surely wisdom and compassion shall follow me
    all the days of my life;
And I shall live with my children in the love of the Lord forever.
                                     Amen.

Children are a gift from the LORD; they are a reward from him.
   Psalm 127:3 NLT

The father of godly children has cause for joy. What a pleasure to have children who are wise.
   Proverbs 23:24 NLT

Yet, O LORD, you are our Father. We are the clay, you are the potter; we are all the work of your hand.
   Isaiah 64:8 NIV

For Celebrating Family

The Lord is generous, we shall not want for love of family.

He makes us hold close children born of His love;
   He tells us of knowing them before they were born.

He guides us to be the hand of compassion to the
   child who is lost, the nurse for the child who is hurting,
   the advocate for the child who has no one
   to speak for him.
For all these precious gifts, we are grateful unto the Lord.

Yea, though we walk through the valleys of doubt and
   disappointment, we shall cherish our family
   for You have wonderfully made us.

You prepare a feast for our family,
   in the presence of those who would love us most.
You anoint our heads with peace; our joy is abundantly
   renewed in You.

Surely mercy and blessings shall follow us
   as long as we live;
And we shall dwell in the family of God forever.

Amen.

For the sake of my family and friends, I will say, May you have peace.

Psalm 122:8 NLT

And how happy I was with the world he created; how I rejoiced with the human family!

Proverbs 8:31 NLT

For My Desire for Intimacy

The Lord is my most beloved,
   I shall not walk in the shadows.

He makes me to marry with the soft promise of love;
He leads me beside a gentle partner
   who will become the parent of my children.

He restores my faith in relationship.
He leads me in the paths of godliness
   so my love will speak louder than words.

Yea, though I walk through the shadow
   of the valley of doubt, I shall fear no uncertainty,
   for You are with me.
Your assurance and your unwavering belief sustain me.

You prepare a wedding banquet for me
   in the presence of family and friends.
You anoint my intimate moments with love;
   my gratitude overflows.

Surely your loving arms will hold me
   all the days of my life;
And I will live within the intimacy
   of the Lord's house forever.

Amen.

The kingdom of heaven is like a king who prepared a wedding banquet for his son.

Matthew 22:2 NIV

As God's partners, we beg you not to accept this marvelous gift of God's kindness and then ignore it.

2 Corinthians 6:1 NLT

So we ourselves should support them so that we can be their partners as they teach the truth.

3 John 1:8 NLT

For we know that if our earthly house, this tent, is destroyed, we have a building from God, a house not made with hands, eternal in the heavens.

2 Corinthians 5:1 NKJV

೫০ For My Need for Companionship ೧৪

The Lord is my companion, I shall not be left alone.

He asks me to sit with him on the edge of the sea
    while we listen to the soft lapping of water on wood.

He restores my hope in faithfulness,
    for He leaves me not.
He leads me in paths of right being
    so I may be a friend to those in need.

Yea, though I walk through the solitary plain of discontent,
    I refuse to feel alone.
For You are by my side within my loneliness;
    Your very presence comforts me greatly.

You prepare a table for me in the presence
    of your invited guests.
You anoint my head with the oil of your harvest
    and the wine of your vine.
I can no longer pretend that my cup is filled by me alone.

Surely friendship and relationship
    shall forever be my gifts;
And I shall live in companionship with the Lord
    in all ways.

Amen.

Right now you have plenty and can help those who are in need. Later, they will have plenty and can share with you when you need it. In this way, things will be equal.

2 Corinthians 8:14 NLT

For if either of them falls, the one will lift up his companion. But woe to the one who falls when there is not an other to lift him up.

Ecclesiastes 4:10 NASB

Our great desire is that you will keep on loving others as long as life lasts, in order to make certain that what you hope for will come true.

Hebrews 6:11 NLT

༝ For Gratitude for Animal Companions ༝

For God so loves the world, He gives us animal companions.

The Lord is creator of all,
  His animals give us their unconditional love.
He makes them to run free in green fields;
  He makes them lie down to nap in the sun.
He leads them to swim in still waters
  until they are exhausted with joy.

He renews their love daily so they may give to us,
  and we shall give to others.
Praise God for giving us such loving creatures in our
  larger world, for it is a better place because of them.

Yea, though our companions live in a world sometimes
  rocked with peril, they fear not, for their boundless love
  compels them to give us their all, even unto death.
Their love and their loyalty comfort us.

You prepare a special place for animals in the presence
  of those who love them;
You lead them to the human who needs them.
You anoint them with special gifts: to lead the blind,
  to protect the sick, to find the lost child,
  to nurture the old, to display extraordinary courage to save
  the human they love.

Surely your goodness shall follow the animals
  all the days of their lives;
And they will companion us forever.

Amen.

You are to bring into the ark two of all living creatures, male and female, to keep them alive with you.

Genesis 6:19 NIV

And be sure to take on board enough food for your family and for all the animals.

Genesis 6:21 NLT

A Prayer for Our Children

The Lord is every child's Father,
   the children shall not want.

He makes them to play in times of playfulness;
He places prayer upon their lips
   before they learn to speak.
He leads them into the stillness of his embrace and
   He waits for them there.

He remembers their infant souls and leads them in paths
   of maturity and courage; He leaves them not.

Yea, though they walk through the halls of indecision,
   they shall choose wisely for You are with them.
Though they do not yet know your master plan,
   your gentle relationship calms and comforts
   and encourages the timid soul.

You prepare a table for them in the presence
   of all fathers and mothers.
You anoint their young heads with vigor and faith;
   your protection spills over on their child-like ways.

Surely goodness and grace shall follow them
   all the days of their lives;
And they shall be counted as God's children forever.

Amen.

He said to them, "Let the little children come to me, and do not hinder them, for the kingdom of God belongs to such as these."
Mark 10:14 NIV

One day some parents brought their children to Jesus so he could lay his hands on them and pray for them.
Matthew 19:13 NLT

I have no greater joy than to hear that my children are walking in the truth.
3 John 1:4 NIV

☙ A Vision of Peace ❧

The Lord is our peacemaker, we shall not hate.

He makes us to lie down as lambs with the lion.
He leads us beside the world's diversity,
    while filling us with His love.

He restores our hope for a world without war;
He leads us in paths of right choices
    as we hold his Holy name in prayer.

Yea, though we walk through a world rife with violence,
    we will not be afraid.
For we are the new peacemakers and You are with us.
Your gifts of faith, hope and love, they comfort us all.

You prepare for us a heavenly kingdom
    where peace will reign, for love conquers all.
You anoint our lives with peace; our cups run over.

Surely peace and harmony will be with us always;
And we will live with the Lord, our God, forever.
                               Amen.

Are we not all children of the same Father?
Are we not all created by the same God?
Then why do we betray each other, violating the covenant of our ancestors?

Malachi 2:10 NLT

Blessed are the peacemakers, for they will be called sons of God.

Matthew 5:9 NIV

Peace I leave with you; my peace I give you.
I do not give to you as the world gives.
Do not let your hearts be troubled and do not be afraid.

John 14:27 NIV

༄ For Appreciation of Beauty ༂

The Lord opens my eyes, I shall not want for beauty.

He makes me lie down in beds of wild roses;
    He leads me beside blooms where butterflies drink.

He restores my belief in goodness;
    He lifts my eyes to the heavens.
He leads me through fields of lavender;
    He decorates my soul.
I praise His name today, tomorrow and always.

Yea, though I walk over barren ground thick with thorns,
    I will fear no harshness;
    for your fertile word is within me.
Your soft wind and warm rain, they comfort me.

You prepare a banquet for me
    in the midst of those who seek your beauty.
You anoint my face with ancient oils,
    my sense of your bounty spills into praise.

Surely beauty and loveliness shall nourish me
    all the days of my life;
And I will live in awe of God's wondrous beauty forever.
                                  Amen.

He searches the sources of the rivers and brings hidden things to light.

Job 28:11 NIV

As the light approaches, the earth takes shape like clay pressed beneath a seal; it is robed in brilliant color.

Job 38:14 NLT

The grasslands of the wilderness become a lush pasture, and the hillsides blossom with joy.

Psalm 65:12 NLT

৯০ A Prayer for Honoring the Earth ৫৫

The Lord is the earth's shepherd,
  we shall honor our home.

He makes us to plant seed in green pastures;
  He leads us to keep the still waters clean.

He restores our collective soul;
  He leads us in paths of right doing for His name's sake.

Yea, though we walk through the valley tarnished by man,
  we shall fear no desolation,
  for You are the master of resurrection.
Your way and your Word, they comfort and collect us.

You prepare our hearts to think globally
  in the presence of those who would think small.
You anoint the heads of your people
  with the wisdom of the ancients; we will nurture our earth.

Surely the earth's prayer shall develop within us;
And we shall dwell in the grace of our God forever.
Amen.

God called the dry ground land, and the gathered waters he called seas. And God saw that it was good.

The land produced vegetation: plants bearing seed according to their kinds and trees bearing fruit with seed in it according to their kinds.

And God saw that it was good.

Genesis 1:10,12 NIV

Praise him, sun and moon, praise him, all you shining stars.
Praise him, you highest heavens and you waters above the skies.

Psalm 148:3 NIV

Let them praise the name of the LORD, for his name alone is exalted; his splendor is above the earth and the heavens.

Psalm 148:13 NIV

You take care of the earth and water it, making it rich and fertile. The river of God has plenty of water; it provides a bountiful harvest of grain, for you have ordered it so.

Psalm 65:9 NLT

࿐ For Raising My Spirits with the Gift of Song ࿐

The Lord is my composer, I shall not be without hymns.

He makes me to sing so I might know Him more;
   He leads me beside the lake of soulful songs.

He renews my soul with peace, for when I sing
   the burden is light, my courage is great, my anxiety no more.
He guides me with notes that are the music of God.

Yea, though I walk through the desert that sings no song,
   I will fear no silence, for your word uplifts my voice
   and sets my feet in harmony.

You prepare a symphony so that I may give voice
   to my deepest feelings;
   You anoint my head with Angel tones.
My cup bursts open with joyful song.

Surely music and song shall follow me in all ways;
And we will live in the heart of the Lord's song forever.
                                          Amen.

I will praise you with the harp for your faithfulness, O my God; I will sing praise to you with the lyre, O Holy One of Israel.

Psalm 71:22 NIV

For You have been my help, And in the shadow of Your wings I sing for joy.

Psalm 63:7 NASB

You will go out in joy and be led forth in peace; the mountains and hills will burst into song before you, and all the trees of the field will clap their hands.

Isaiah 55:12 NIV

But the fruit of the Spirit is love, joy, peace, patience, kindness, goodness, faithfulness, gentleness and self-control.
Galatians 5:22 NIV

In all my prayers for all of you, I always pray with joy.
Philippians 1:4 NIV

ॐ With Gratitude ॐ

To all who have been part of my spiritual journey,
I am thankful for your love and support.
I would especially like to thank Linda for
giving me her gifts of organization and design
in preparing this book.

~ Peggy

I welcome your comments and stories.
You may email me at peggyjmcmahon@gmail.com